What's in this book

This book belongs to

_____

健康饮食 Healthy eating

学习内容 Contents

沟通 Communication

说说食物
Talk about food

提供健康饮食的建议
Give suggestions on
healthy eating

生词 New words

★ 鸡蛋	egg
★ 三明治	sandwich
★ 蔬菜	vegetable
★ 米饭	rice
★ 饿	hungry
★ 饼干	biscuit
★ 巧克力	chocolate
★ 别	do not
薯条	potato chip
薯片	potato crisp
汉堡包	hamburger
冰淇淋	ice cream
这些	these

句式 Sentence patterns

多吃蔬菜、水果，多喝水。
Eat more vegetables and fruit. Drink more water.

别吃太多汉堡包。
Do not eat too many hamburgers.

文化 Cultures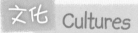

汉字"菜"的演变
The evolution of the
Chinese character 菜

跨学科学习 Project

认识健康饮食，设计健康菜单
Learn about healthy diets and
design a healthy menu

Get ready

1 Do you enjoy eating?

2 What is your favourite food?

3 Do you think you have a healthy diet?

jī dàn
鸡蛋

早上，我们喜欢吃鸡蛋和水果、喝果汁。

蔬菜

sān míng zhì
三明治

中午，我们喜欢吃三明治和蔬菜。

mǐ fàn
米饭

è
饿

晚上，我们喜欢吃米饭。你肚子
饿了吃什么？

汉堡包、薯条、薯片？饼干、
巧克力、冰淇淋？

zhè xiē
这些

多吃蔬菜和水果，这些食物很健康。
多喝水。

别吃太多零食和汉堡包，这些食物
不健康。

Let's think

1 Recall the story. Draw the food items that we should eat less of in the circle.

多吃

少吃

2 What do you eat at lunch? Draw your meal and discuss with your friend whether it is healthy.

New words

1 Learn the new words.

鸡蛋

米饭

蔬菜 这些

三明治

饼干

巧克力

汉堡包

薯条

薯片

冰淇淋

饿

别

2 Listen to your teacher and point to the correct words above.

听听说说 Listen and say

🎧 03 **1** Listen and circle the correct answers.

🎧 04 **2** Look at the pictures. Listen to the story c

1 女孩中午吃了什么？

   a   糖果

   b   三明治

   c   苹果

2 男孩怎么了？

   a   他饿了。

   b   他累了。

   c   他来了。

3 姐姐说别吃什么？

   a   鸡蛋

   b   蔬菜

   c   巧克力

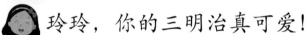
玲玲，你的三明治真可爱！

谢谢。你也喜欢这些鸡蛋吗？

因为他是"蔬菜水果人"，所以他的身体很好。

y.

我是谁?

你是"巧克力饼干人"。

别玩了。你们不饿吗?快吃吧。

3 **Complete the sentences.**
Role-play with your friend.

我喜欢吃……
我的朋友喜欢
吃……

我吃很多……
我不吃……

我们最好多吃……
别吃太多……
我们也要多喝……
我们的身体……

Task

Plan a Healthy Eating Week in your class. Draw the posters and talk about them.

Game

Talk about the fruit and vegetables. Find ten differences between the pictures and circle them on the right picture.

Chant

05 Listen and say.

三明治、水果和牛奶，
蔬菜、米饭和鸡蛋，
这些食物多吃点。

汉堡包、薯条和薯片，
冰淇淋和巧克力，
这些食物少吃点。

吃得健康，身体健康，
快快乐乐真开心。

生活用语 Daily expressions

好吃!
It's delicious!

别说了。
Stop talking.

写一写 Write

1 Trace and write the characters.

丿 一 亅 手 我 我 我

我 我 我 我

丿 亅 亇 亇 亇 竹 饣 饿 饿 饿

饿 饿 饿 饿

2 Write and say.

中午，___饿了，我吃三明治和水果。

_____，我___了，我吃米饭和蔬菜。

3 Fill in the blanks with the correct words. Colour the empty plates using the same colours.

你＿＿＿，这些脸都会＿＿＿，它们真可爱。现在，你＿＿＿了吗？

你喜欢吃三明治还是鸡蛋？你喜欢吃蔬菜和＿＿＿＿＿＿吗？

拼音输入法 Pinyin input

It is important to remember the Pinyin spelling rules. When 'j', 'q', 'x' and 'y' are in front of 'ü', 'ü' should be changed to 'u'. We should also type 'u' instead of 'ü' in these cases.

1 Circle the correct answers for inputting these characters.

ju	jü	jv	
1 具	2 据	3 句	4 居 ⬆⬇

qü	qv	qu	
1 去	2 区	3 取	4 曲 ⬆⬇

xve	xüe	xue	
1 学	2 雪	3 血	4 穴 ⬆⬇

yuen	yüan	yuan	
1 圆	2 元	3 原	4 远 ⬆⬇

2 Circle the correct answer for inputting 女.

Type 'v' to represent 'ü' when the letters in front of 'ü' are NOT 'j', 'q', 'x' and 'y'.

nü	nu	nv	
1 女			⬆⬇

Cultures

1 Learn about the evolution of the character 菜.

A long time ago, the character 菜 only referred to the plants that are picked from the fields and eaten as food.

Later, it would be used to refer to a dish (e.g. 炒菜) which is made with vegetables, meat or eggs.

Now, the character has an even wider meaning. It can even be used to talk about cuisines (e.g. 中国菜).

2 There are over 600 kinds of vegetables in Chinese cuisine. Look at the ones below. Write the letters in the correct boxes.

a Aubergine b Chinese cabbage c Ginger d Choy sum

1 Find out what a balanced diet consists of and what junk food we should eat less.

Balanced diet

Junk food

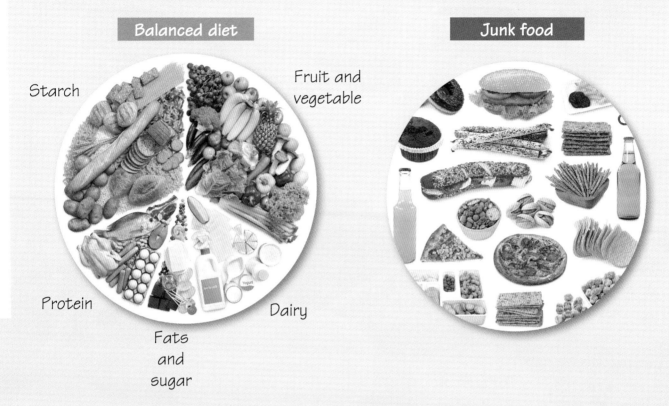

Starch

Fruit and vegetable

Protein

Dairy

Fats and sugar

2 Design a healthy breakfast, lunch and dinner for yourself. Draw and tell your friends.

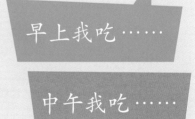

早上我吃……

中午我吃……

多吃蔬菜和水果!

晚上我吃……

温习 Checkpoint

1 Role-play with your friends. Point to the food when you act it out.

我饿了！我们去吃什么？

我吃蔬菜和米饭。

我吃三明治和水果。

我喝水。

我们吃汉堡包和巧克力蛋糕。

我们最喜欢吃鸡蛋。

了！

我喝苹果茶。

别吃那些。我们多吃蔬菜、多喝水，身体好。

2 Work with your friend. Colour the stars and the chilies.

Words	说	读	写
鸡蛋	☆	☆	🌶
三明治	☆	☆	🌶
蔬菜	☆	☆	🌶
米饭	☆	☆	🌶
饿	☆	☆	☆
饼干	☆	☆	🌶
巧克力	☆	☆	🌶
别	☆	☆	🌶
汉堡包	☆	🌶	🌶
薯条	☆	🌶	🌶
薯片	☆	🌶	🌶

Words and sentences	说	读	写
冰淇淋	☆	🌶	🌶
这些	☆	🌶	🌶
我们喜欢吃鸡蛋和水果。	☆	☆	🌶
多吃蔬菜、水果，多喝水。	☆	☆	🌶
别吃太多汉堡包。	☆	🌶	🌶

Say the names of food items	☆
Give suggestions on healthy eating	☆

3 What does your teacher say?

My teacher says ...

分享 Sharing

Words I remember

鸡蛋	jī dàn	egg
三明治	sān míng zhì	sandwich
蔬菜	shū cài	vegetables
米饭	mǐ fàn	rice
饿	è	hungry
饼干	bǐng gān	biscuit
巧克力	qiǎo kè lì	chocolate
别	bié	do not
汉堡包	hàn bǎo bāo	hamburger
薯条	shǔ tiáo	potato chip
薯片	shǔ piàn	potato crisp
冰淇淋	bīng qí lín	ice cream
这些	zhè xiē	these

Other words

肚子	dù zi	stomach
食物	shí wù	food
健康	jiàn kāng	healthy
太多	tài duō	too many, too much
零食	líng shí	snack
让	ràng	to allow

OXFORD
UNIVERSITY PRESS

Oxford University Press is a department of the University of Oxford.
It furthers the University's objective of excellence in research, scholarship,
and education by publishing worldwide. Oxford is a registered trade mark of
Oxford University Press in the UK and in certain other countries

Published in Hong Kong by
Oxford University Press (China) Limited
39th Floor, One Kowloon, 1 Wang Yuen Street, Kowloon Bay,
Hong Kong

Illustrated by Anne Lee and Wildman

Photographs for reproduction permitted by Dreamstime.com

China National Publications Import & Export (Group) Corporation is an authorized distributor of
Oxford Elementary Chinese.

Please contact content@cnpiec.com.cn or 86-10-65856782

ISBN: 978019-082252-1

10 9 8 7 6 5 4 3 2